AF481097

TABLE OF CONTENTS

Any leftover potatoes can be used (tator tots, mashed potatoes, sunrise/baby potatoes, au gratin leftover, chopped up baked potato remnants, ANY sort of potato)

INTRO & DEDICATION

For all the folks out there who thought you couldn't use leftover french fries & tator tots; green salad, or days-old grill burgers & dogs – look no further than this crafty guide from a new mother, new to city-homesteading, and a true lady. Accustomed to luxury, boutique food & travel, willfully stuck at home with two young kids yet wanting to eat meals on a daily basis that take her back to her 30's, spent in NYC with her husband eating every meal out, she's come up with ways to use mundane leftovers and turn them into trendy-restaurant quality dishes! This is the second book of The Raw Milkmaid's City Homesteader Series – watch out for more to come!

<u>Home Chef Tip:</u>
If you're short on ideas and meal planning for the week, simply scan both of these menus, cook one dish, then use the leftovers for the next dish… be creative and make it fun, make it "YOURS", and find your cooking skills escalate in the process!

●Follow:
@catdevinezagorski
@devinecooks
@the_raw_milkmaid
@the_water_priestess
●Photography:
@devinelifenyc @hizherztravelz

To The Great Cosmic Mother: I AM Your Vessel; mold me, use me. To my beloved, Michael, and to our earth angels, MM & MJ – Everything I do is for you and our sacred bond.

LEFTOVER FRENCH FRIES/TATOR TOTS

INTO

BREAKFAST OR DINNER POTATO MASH

INGREDIENTS:

Prep Time: 10 Min
Total Time: 20 Min

- Leftover potatoes; any kind, any quantity
- Heavy cream (preferably raw, enough to coat mixture and reconstitute mixture)
- Maldon pyramid salt flakes (to taste)
- Black pepper to taste
- Shredded cheese (cheddar, or any kind you have available)
- Chives, rosemary, any similar herbs laying around
- Butter or oil of choice (garlic infused olive oil is my fav!)
- Sweet onions, chopped (about a handful per leftover cup of potatoes)
- Garlic, tomatoes, leftover peppers/veggies, and other ingredients can be added, depending on your mood and inventory!

- *See the back section of this book for my 'necessary' luxury ingredients, which really make these into top-tier restaurant meals*

LEFTOVER FRENCH FRIES/TATOR TOTS

INTO

BREAKFAST OR DINNER POTATO MASH

STEPS TO PREPARE:

1. Take leftover potatoes and get them ready to sauté. Using kitchen scissors or a knife, chop fries into bite size pieces, cut tator tots in half, even mashed potatoes can be used.
2. Add butter or oil of choice to pan, and toss in chopped sweet onions, sauté about 3-5 min. on medium.
3. Toss in leftover potatoes with some herbs, and other veggies (anything you desire to add), along with heavy cream, salt and pepper. Combine all ingredients and sauté until any excess liquid is evaporated, and there is just enough to toss some shredded cheese into the mix. Swirl cheese around entire mixture, put heat on low/warm, and cover until ready to eat.

- *See the back section of this book for my 'necessary' luxury ingredients, which really make these into top-tier restaurant meals*

LEFTOVER BEEF/PORK ROAST

INTO

PULLED BEEF/PORK TACOS

INGREDIENTS:

Prep Time: 10 Min
Total Time: 20 Min

- Leftover beef or pork roast (any meat really)
- Beef or chicken stock, water, milk, cream, or most any other liquid you have available (used to reconstitute the meat and create a tasty sauce)
- Taco seasoning, or chili spice, garlic, white pepper, black pepper, salt, cilantro or basil, chives, most any leftover herbs will work. Add to taste, start small and add more as needed
- Shredded cheese (cheddar, or any kind you have available, enough to dress tacos
- Tortillas (flour or corn)
- Taco dressings: as desired (fresh tomatoes, corn, lettuce, sour cream, onion, shredded cheese, etc.)
- Dash with some Brightland chili olive oil
- Squeeze of lime

- *See the back section of this book for my 'necessary' luxury ingredients, which really make these into top-tier restaurant meals*

LEFTOVER BEEF/PORK ROAST

INTO

PULLED BEEF/PORK TACOS

STEPS TO PREPARE:

1. Take leftover beef/pork roast and, while cold, pull apart along the grain of the meat, or cut using kitchen scissors, using any leftover drippings, warm in a pan on medium. Add beef or chicken stock, water, milk, cream, or most any other liquid you have leftover – and reheat the meat.
2. Add taco seasoning, or chili spice, garlic, white pepper, black pepper, salt, cilantro or basil, chives, most any leftover herbs will work.
3. Warm tortillas in oven (covered in pan or wrapped in tin foil, low or warm for 5 minutes).
4. Dress as desired (fresh tomatoes, corn, lettuce, sour cream, shredded cheese, etc.) and dash with some Brightland chili olive oil, and a squeeze of lime.

- *See the back section of this book for my 'necessary' luxury ingredients, which really make these into top-tier restaurant meals*

LEFTOVER GRILLED/BOILED HOTDOGS

INTO

WEENIES & RICE W/ VEGGIES, BASIL OIL, CREAM

INGREDIENTS:

Prep Time: 5 Min
Total Time: 10 Min

- Leftover grilled or boiled hotdogs
- Organic Indian Basmati is preferred (but any white rice will do), also adding some minced garlic and butter while preparing elevates the taste, but is not necessary. Add 2 cups water for each cup of rice (depends on amount of leftovers)
- 2 tablespoons butter per cup of rice
- Touch of heavy cream
- Maldon Salt
- Dash of Brightland Basil Olive Oil (any flavored olive oil)
- Leftover peppers, onions, or any other veggie laying around, if interested, just enough for some extra flavor

- *See the back section of this book for my 'necessary' luxury ingredients, which really make these into top-tier restaurant meals*

LEFTOVER GRILLED/BOILED HOTDOGS

INTO

WEENIES & RICE W/ VEGGIES, BASIL OIL, CREAM

STEPS TO PREPARE:

1. Use kitchen scissors or knife to cut hot dogs into bitesize pieces.
2. Cook rice according to package (use 2 cups water for every 1 cup of rice) in a medium pot – Organic Indian Basmati is wonderful, also adding some minced garlic and butter while preparing elevates the taste.
3. Melt 2 tablespoons of butter in the rice, and toss in hot dogs.
4. Stir in a touch of heavy cream, Maldon Salt, a dash of Brightland Basil Olive Oil (any flavored olive oil).
5. You can add in leftover peppers, onions, or any other veggie laying around, if interested.

- *See the back section of this book for my 'necessary' luxury ingredients, which really make these into top-tier restaurant meals*

LEFTOVER GRILL BURGERS

INTO

BEEF & VEGGIE WHITE PASTA

INGREDIENTS:

Prep Time: 10 Min
Total Time: 25 Min

- Leftover grilled burgers
- Approx. 2-4 cups heavy cream (depends how much beef is leftover)
- 2 tablespoons butter per 2 cups cream
- 1 tablespoon Brigtland Rapture Balsamic Vinegar
- Maldon Salt
- Dash of Brightland Basil Olive Oil (any flavored olive oil)
- Leftover peppers or any other veggie laying around, if interested
- ½ - 1 sweet onion
- Any other veggies laying around (broccoli, mushrooms, etc.)
- 2-4 tablespoons agave
- Black pepper to taste
- Extra salad dressings laying around (vinegar based)(optional)
- Fresh herbs/spices of choice (optional)
- Shredded cheese to top (optional)

- *See the back section of this book for my 'necessary' luxury ingredients, which really make these into top-tier restaurant meals*

LEFTOVER GRILL BURGERS

INTO

BEEF & VEGGIE WHITE PASTA

STEPS TO PREPARE:

1. Use kitchen scissors or knife to cut leftover burgers into bitesize pieces, crumbling if possible (not necessary).
2. Sauté butter, onions, peppers, desired spices, vinegar, and cream, on medium heat. Let simmer until desired consistency is reached.
3. Boil water, cook pasta in a large pot – fresh pasta really elevates this dish!
4. Stir in any cheese, Maldon Salt, a dash of Brightland Basil Olive Oil (any flavored olive oil), and cover on low. Ready to eat when desired thickness is reached.
5. Strain pasta, then stir into thickened sauce. Serve, topped with shredded cheese and black pepper (as optional, above).

- *See the back section of this book for my 'necessary' luxury ingredients, which really make these into top-tier restaurant meals*

LEFTOVER PORK/BEEF CHUCK ROLL

INTO

CHEESESTEAK SUBS

Prep Time: 15 Min
Total Time: 25 Min

INGREDIENTS:

- Leftover pork/beef chuck roll
- Approx. 2-4 cups heavy cream (depends how much beef is leftover)
- Beef stock (chicken stock can be used in a pinch), approx. 2 tbsp for each 2 cups cream
- Maldon Salt
- Black pepper to taste
- Green peppers (1/2 to 1 pepper)
- Sweet onions (1/2 to 1 onion)
- Mayonnaise (swipe on bread)
- Shredded cheese to top
- Lettuce, tomato to top sub

- *See the back section of this book for my 'necessary' luxury ingredients, which really make these into top-tier restaurant meals*

LEFTOVER PORK/BEEF CHUCK ROLL

INTO

CHEESESTEAK SUBS

STEPS TO PREPARE:

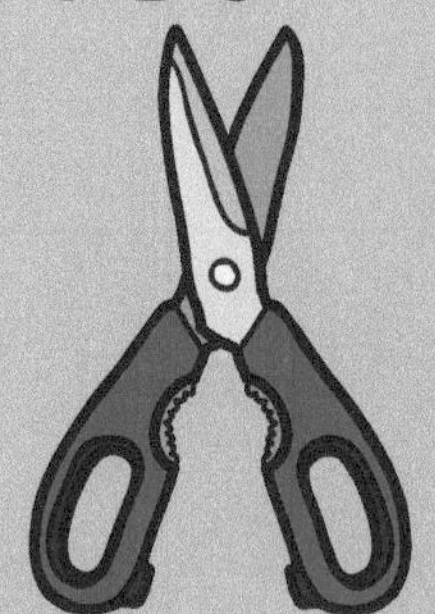

1. Use kitchen scissors or knife to cut leftover chuck roll into thin long pieces, cutting/pulling along the grain of meat.
2. Sauté cream, onions, peppers, desired spices, vinegar, and meat, on medium heat. Let simmer until meat is warmed up.
3. Warm rolls in the oven, covered, so they are soft. Dash with mayo and top with meat/pepper/onion mixture. Serve.

- *See the back section of this book for my 'necessary' luxury ingredients, which really make these into top-tier restaurant meals*

LEFTOVER TACO MEAT

INTO

SPICY BEEF PASTA, RED/VODKA SAUCE

INGREDIENTS:

Prep Time: 10 Min
Total Time: 25 Min

- Leftover taco meat
- Approx. 1/2 cup heavy cream (depends how much beef is leftover)
- 1 bottle pasta sauce (Rao's vodka sauce is a favorite, and my hometown favorite is Bombolini)
- 1 tablespoon Brightland Rapture Balsamic Vinegar
- Maldon Salt
- Dash of Brightland Basil Olive Oil (any flavored olive oil)
- Leftover peppers or any other veggie laying around, if interested
- ½ - 1 sweet onion
- 2-4 tablespoons agave
- Garlic minced (optional)
- Black pepper to taste
- Fresh herbs/spices of choice (optional)
- Shredded cheese to top (optional)

- *See the back section of this book for my 'necessary' luxury ingredients, which really make these into top-tier restaurant meals*

LEFTOVER TACO MEAT

INTO

SPICY BEEF PASTA, RED/VODKA SAUCE

STEPS TO PREPARE:

1. Use kitchen scissors or knife to cut leftover burgers into bitesize pieces, crumbling if possible (not necessary).
2. Sauté, leftover meat, onions, peppers/veggies of choice, desired spices, cream, and agave, on medium heat. Add red/vodka sauce; let simmer until desired consistency is reached.
3. Boil water, cook pasta of choice in a large pot – fresh pasta really elevates this dish!
4. Stir in any cheese, Maldon Salt, a dash of Brightland Basil Olive Oil (any flavored olive oil like garlic), and cover on low. Ready to eat when desired thickness is reached.
5. Strain pasta, then stir into thickened sauce. Serve.

- *See the back section of this book for my 'necessary' luxury ingredients, which really make these into top-tier restaurant meals*

LEFTOVER GREEN SALAD

INTO

QUINOA, BALSAMIC, BASIL OLIVE OIL, HERBS & VEGGIES

INGREDIENTS:

Prep Time: 5 Min
Total Time: 10 Min

- Leftover green salad
- 1 bag frozen quinoa, or dry can be used, depending on how much salad is leftover
- 1 tablespoon Brightland Rapture Balsamic Vinegar, or more depending on leftovers
- Maldon Salt
- Dash of Brightland Basil Olive Oil (any flavored olive oil)
- Leftover peppers or any other veggie laying around, if interested
- ½ - 1 sweet onion
- Black pepper to taste
- Fresh herbs/spices of choice (optional)
- Chicken breast or other protein (optional)

- *See the back section of this book for my 'necessary' luxury ingredients, which really make these into top-tier restaurant meals*

LEFTOVER GREEN SALAD

INTO

QUINOA,
BALSAMIC, BASIL OLIVE OIL,
HERBS & VEGGIES

STEPS TO PREPARE:

1. Boil water for quinoa per instructions on bag; add Maldon salt to taste.
2. Chop onions, veggies, herbs, almost anything laying around can be added!
3. Take cooked quinoa, stir in leftover salad, and all chopped onions/veggies/herbs.
4. Top with cracked black pepper, Maldon Salt, a dash of Brightland Basil or Garlic Olive Oil (any flavored olive oil), and Brightland Rapture Balsamic Vinegar.
5. Serve as a delicious side dish, or meal. Add chicken or protein if desired!

- *See the back section of this book for my 'necessary' luxury ingredients, which really make these into top-tier restaurant meals*

LEFTOVER PASTA & SAUCE

INTO

HOMEMADE PIZZAS

INGREDIENTS:

Prep Time: 10 Min
Total Time: 20 Min

- Leftover pasta sauce, with or without pasta still included. The number of pizzas you can make depends on the volume of sauce.
- Naan, flatbread, or pizza crust of choice
- Shredded cheese of choice (I prefer sharp cheddar)
- Sprinkle of Brightland Rapture Balsamic Vinegar, or more depending on leftovers
- Maldon Salt
- Dash of Brightland Basil Olive Oil (any flavored olive oil)
- Leftover peppers or any other veggie laying around, if desired
- ½ - 1 sweet onion
- Black pepper to taste
- Fresh herbs/spices of choice (optional)
- Agave or honey (optional)

- *See the back section of this book for my 'necessary' luxury ingredients, which really make these into top-tier restaurant meals*

LEFTOVER PASTA & SAUCE

INTO

HOMEMADE PIZZAS

STEPS TO PREPARE:

1. Take naan, flatbread, or pizza crust of choice, and take leftover sauce (if pasta is still included, cut it up very well), to cover bread, leaving only room for crust.
2. Preheat oven to approx. 425 degrees.
3. Chop onions, veggies, herbs, almost anything leftover can be added.
4. Sprinkle cheese, veggies, and all other ingredients onto pizza.
5. Top with cracked black pepper, Maldon Salt, a dash of Brightland Basil or Garlic Olive Oil (any flavored olive oil), and Brightland Rapture Balsamic Vinegar. Also a dash of agave or honey elevates the dish!
6. Bake for approx. 7-10 min. until desired crunchiness.

- *See the back section of this book for my 'necessary' luxury ingredients, which really make these into top-tier restaurant meals*

LEFTOVER CHICKEN TENDERS

INTO

SWEET & SPICY LETTUCE WRAPS

INGREDIENTS:

Prep Time: 10 Min
Total Time: 15 Min

- Leftover chicken nuggets (breaded or unbreaded chicken can be used)
- Honey for texture and taste (I prefer an orange blossom honey from Brightland)
- 1 Tbsp agave
- Spicy/hot sauce of choice, or soy sauce (chipotle habanero and soy mixed together is m favorite, or Ponzu sauce as well; get creative!)
- Maldon Salt
- Cracked black pepper to taste
- 1 tsp butter or oil
- 1 cup sweet onions (more if you have a lot of chicken)
- Scallions/chives to taste
- Romaine, butter, (or any large) lettuce, broken into one piece 'lettuce boats' which can be wrapped like a taco
- Cheese or other desired toppings (optional)

- *See the back section of this book for my 'necessary' luxury ingredients, which really make these into top-tier restaurant meals*

This lettuce was grown in my garden, and was the largest head I've ever seen! Hence the idea for these wraps... keeps lettuce from wasting!

LEFTOVER CHICKEN TENDERS

INTO

SWEET & SPICY LETTUCE WRAPS

STEPS TO PREPARE:

1. Cut up leftover chicken tenders/nuggets with kitchen scissors, bitesized pieces.
2. Saute onions, scallions in butter or oil.
3. Add all other ingredients to pan, until dissolved and a sweet spicy dressing appears.
4. Pull apart lettuce leaves and set aside on plates.
5. Dress the lettuce leaves with chicken/sauce concoction, or serve in a small bowl beside lettuce leaves.

- *See the back section of this book for my 'necessary' luxury ingredients, which really make these into top-tier restaurant meals*

BATCH OF BAKED DOZEN EGGS

INTO

EVERYDAY EGG SAMMIES

INGREDIENTS:

Prep Time: 2 Min
Total Time: 12 Min

As Leftover: 5 Min

- 1 dozen eggs, farm fresh (unwashed) if possible when procured (wash before making)
- ½ cup heavy cream, farm fresh if possible (milk can substitute if needed)
- Shredded cheese of choice (I prefer sharp cheddar)
- Maldon Salt
- Black pepper
- Fresh herbs/spices of choice (optional); my favorite is fresh chives or rosemary
- Mayo, or any flavored aioli for an up kick
- Brioche bread (my favorite), or any bread, roll, biscuit, bagel, muffin, croissant, tortilla, etc.

- *See the back section of this book for my 'necessary' luxury ingredients, which really make these into top-tier restaurant meals*

Shown with brioche above, and a tortilla below; the possibilities are endless!

BATCH OF BAKED DOZEN EGGS

INTO

EVERYDAY EGG SAMMIES

STEPS TO PREPARE:

1. Preheat oven to approx. 350 degrees.
2. Brush olive oil onto a 9x13 baking dish.
3. Crack one dozen eggs into a large bowl, adding the heavy cream.
4. Beat, add Maldon salt, cracked black pepper.
5. Chop onions, veggies, herbs, almost anything leftover can be added, or omit this step.
6. Sprinkle cheese (raw cheddar is my favorite), combine, pour into baking dish, using rubber spatula.
7. Bake for approx. 7-10 min. until eggs are soft and formed; they will taste light and fluffy all week.
8. Reheating is easy – Preheat oven to approx. 250, and using a covered pan, add any desired bread or roll; warm for 3-5 minutes, and this can be spread with mayo, aioli, honey, or jam once it is warm. As another option, once the oven is preheated per instructions below, you can change oven temp. to 'warm' and allow your breakfast to sit in the oven until you are ready for it.

- *See the back section of this book for my 'necessary' luxury ingredients, which really make these into top-tier restaurant meals*

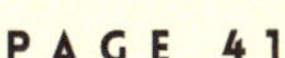

BATCH 1 POUND OF POTATOES

INTO

EVERYDAY POTATOES (ALL MEALS)

Prep Time: 10 Min
Total Time: 35 Min

As Leftover: 5 Min

INGREDIENTS:

- 1 pound of potatoes of choice. Use enough for a large batch of mashed potatoes, which varies based on potato type. I prefer russet or red potatoes for this recipe.
- ½ cup heavy cream, farm fresh if possible (milk can substitute if needed).
- 8 tablespoons butter; enough to coat potatoes, could vary based on first ingredient above and preference.
- Shredded cheese of choice (I prefer sharp cheddar).
- Maldon Salt
- Black pepper
- Fresh herbs/spices of choice (optional); my favorite is fresh chives or rosemary. Also, sweet peppers can be added for a kick!
- ½ cup chopped sweet onions (if being made into breakfast potatoes/hash browns) – omit this if being eaten as a side for lunch or dinner.
- Chives/scallions to taste.

- *See the back section of this book for my 'necessary' luxury ingredients, which really make these into top-tier restaurant meals*

BATCH 1 POUND OF POTATOES

INTO

EVERYDAY POTATOES (SIDE DISH FOR ALL MEALS)

STEPS TO PREPARE:

Making the Batch:
1. Do all beginning steps as if you are making mashed potatoes; chop potatoes and toss into boiling water.
2. Boil 25 minutes or until potatoes are done when poked with a fork.
3. Strain, put back into pot and add butter and Maldon salt.
4. Mash loosely, leaving large chunks so you can utilize these potatoes as you see fit during the week. These can be covered and stored until used, or continue steps below.

Reheating for Daily Potatoes:
1. Chop onions, herbs, toss into medium pan with butter (for breakfast potatoes/hash browns only; omit onions if preparing lunch or dinner potatoes).
2. Simmer on medium until onions are transparent and aromatic; add in leftover potatoes.
3. Add cream, sprinkle cheese, combine, and stir the mixture until desired consistency is met; cover on low temp. until ready to serve. Add further Maldon salt or pepper if desired.
4. Mash further with fork or masher (if desired)if this is for lunch or dinner potatoes.

• *See the back section of this book for my 'necessary' luxury ingredients, which really make these into top-tier restaurant meals*

Breakfast potatoes have sweet onions and a delicious cheesy skillet potato taste!

Dinner potatoes are a simple but perfect creamy mashed potato side dish!

ESSENTIAL LUXURY INGREDIENTS & OTHER TIPS

Essential salt: Maldon Pyramid Sea Salt Flakes – these add a touch (and taste!) of luxury, especially to top soups, burrata/cheese plate, sliced avocado, pastas, potatoes, veggies, meats… anything at ALL. Not only is it delicious to add into the recipe itself (melting flakes into the cooking), but putting a dash on top gives that crunch and flavor from top notch restaurants.

Fresh black pepper: Starwest Botanicals has an incredibly tasty organic black pepper for the grinder.

High quality vinegars, like Brightland's Rapture (a balsamic); they also have champagne, persimmon, and seasonal vinegars that'll knock your socks off!

ESSENTIAL LUXURY
INGREDIENTS & OTHER TIPS

High quality honey: Brightland has a variety of wonderful selections, as well as my ultimate favorite, Flamingo Estates (they curate their honey's based on the moon's cycle and other sacred touches).

High quality herb infused olive oils: Brightland's basil, garlic, rosemary, and lemon olive oils, are a few of my favs! These are great for drizzling over salads and all ingredients, elevating the taste exponentially. On french toast or pancakes, a dash of lemon olive oil and powdered sugar; basil or rosemary oil drizzled over a fresh burrata ball, the list is endless.

Raw Blue Agave: sauces (especially red and white pasta sauces) can be elevated with a 'sweet and spice' touch, by adding agave and a spice or sautéed pepper of choice, also adding ground white pepper gives things a kick.

ESSENTIAL LUXURY
INGREDIENTS & OTHER TIPS

Raw dairy (eggs, cheese, cream and milk): when creating almost anything, using raw dairy takes the flavor and consistency up a few notches, and is basically like using unprocessed dairy which just tastes more wholesome and satisfying.

Fresh herbs preferred over dried.

Fresh pasta preferred over dried; small touches can make a big difference. I buy fresh pasta from our hometown restaurant, Bombolino (supports small businesses AND tastes better, so its a win-win).

TO

www.ingramcontent.com/pod-product-compliance
Lightning Source LLC
Chambersburg PA
CBHW042051100726
47973CB00014B/215